THE MINDFUL YEAR PLANNER

*Transformation doesn't happen all at once ~
it happens one breath, one thoughts, one choice at a time.*

WELCOME, BEAUTIFUL SOUL

YOU ARE HOLDING MORE THAN A PLANNER — YOU'RE HOLDING A JOURNEY.

A SACRED INVITATION TO SLOW DOWN, RECONNECT, AND ALIGN WITH THE TRUEST VERSION OF YOURSELF.

WITHIN THESE PAGES, YOU'LL BE GUIDED THROUGH TWELVE MONTHS OF MINDFUL LIVING — GROUNDED IN GRATITUDE, AWAKENED TO POSSIBILITY, ALIGNED WITH PURPOSE, AND EMBODIED IN JOY.

PILLARS OF TRANSFORMATION:

GROUND — FIND SAFETY, STABILITY, AND GRATITUDE.
AWAKEN — OPEN YOUR MIND, HEART, AND ENERGY TO POSSIBILITY.
MANIFEST — BRING YOUR INTENTIONS INTO FORM THROUGH INSPIRED ACTION.
EVOLVE — FLOW, HEAL, AND GROW WITH GRACE.
CONQUER — STAND IN CONFIDENCE AND EMBODIED STRENGTH.
EMBODY — LIVE IN JOY, AUTHENTICITY, AND ALIGNMENT.

THE MINDFUL YEAR PLANNER

Transformation doesn't happen all at once ~
it happens one breath, one thoughts, one choice at a time.

EACH MONTH INCLUDES SPACE TO:

SET INTENTIONS
PRACTICE GRATITUDE
REFLECT ON GROWTH
RECEIVE DAILY INSPIRATION
RETURN TO PRESENCE

THIS ISN'T ABOUT PERFECTION — IT'S ABOUT PRESENCE.

YOU DON'T NEED TO CONTROL YOUR PATH;
YOU ONLY NEED TO WALK IT WITH AWARENESS.
TAKE A DEEP BREATH.
OPEN YOUR HEART.
YOUR YEAR OF TRANSFORMATION BEGINS NOW.

"THE TRUEJOY JOURNEY ISN'T ABOUT BECOMING SOMEONE NEW — IT'S
ABOUT REMEMBERING WHO YOU ALREADY ARE."

HOW TO USE THIS PLANNER

A mindful guide to getting the most out of your year.

THIS PLANNER IS DESIGNED TO SUPPORT A FULL
YEAR OF MINDFUL LIVING.

IT FLOWS WITH INTENTIONAL STRUCTURE WHILE
LEAVING SPACE FOR YOUR INTUITION AND
PERSONAL RHYTHM.

THERE IS NO "RIGHT WAY" TO USE IT —
ONLY THE WAY THAT FEELS ALIGNED.

REMEMBER:
THIS PLANNER IS YOUR COMPANION, **NOT YOUR CRITIC.**

HOW TO USE THIS PLANNER

USE THIS PLANNER TO:

SET MONTHLY INTENTIONS
ANCHOR INTO DAILY INSPIRATION AND GRATITUDE
REFLECT ON GROWTH EACH MONTH
TRACK YOUR EMOTIONAL, SPIRITUAL, AND PERSONAL
EVOLUTION
STAY ALIGNED WITH THE SIX TRUEJOY LIVING PILLARS

YOUR RHYTHM MIGHT LOOK LIKE:

MORNING: READ YOUR AFFIRMATION OR SET YOUR DAILY
INTENTION
AFTERNOON: PAUSE WITH A "DON'T FORGET" REMINDER
EVENING: REFLECT ON WHAT FELT ALIGNED

REMEMBER:
THIS PLANNER IS YOUR COMPANION, **NOT YOUR CRITIC.**

MY MORNING RITUAL

BEGIN YOUR DAY WITH INTENTION.

MY MORNING INTENTION:

HOW I WANT TO FEEL TODAY:

MOVEMENT / BREATHWORK:

NOURISHMENT RITUAL:

ONE THING I CAN DO TO SUPPORT MYSELF:

MORNING RITUALS SET THE TONE FOR MINDFUL LIVING.

MY EVENING REFLECTION

A GENTLE CLOSE TO THE DAY.

WHAT FELT ALIGNED TODAY?

WHAT CHALLENGED ME AND WHAT DID IT TEACH ME?

SOMETHING I'M GRATEFUL FOR:

A MOMENT THAT MADE ME SMILE:

WHAT ENERGY I'M RELEASING BEFORE SLEEP:

EVERY ENDING IS A QUIET BEGINNING.

MY VISION FOR THE YEAR

WHAT I'M CALLING IN, CREATING, AND BECOMING.

WHAT DOES MY IDEAL YEAR FEEL LIKE?

WHAT AREAS OF MY LIFE AM I READY TO ELEVATE?

WHO AM I BECOMING THIS YEAR?

WHAT HABITS OR ENERGY PATTERNS DO I WANT TO RELEASE?

WHAT EXPERIENCES OR OPPORTUNITIES DO I DESIRE TO ATTRACT?

LET YOUR VISION BE FELT BEFORE IT IS SEEN.

MY WORD OF THE YEAR

THE ENERGY I AM DEVOTED TO.

MY WORD IS: _____

WHY THIS WORD CHOSE ME:

HOW I WILL EMBODY THIS WORD DAILY:

WHAT THIS WORD WANTS ME TO RELEASE:

WHAT THIS WORD WANTS ME TO STEP INTO:

YOUR WORD BECOMES YOUR COMPASS.

January

GROUND IN GRATITUDE

"I BEGIN THIS YEAR ROOTED, CALM, AND CONNECTED TO MY INNER PEACE."

January
GROUND IN GRATITUDE

MONTHLY FOCUS

THIS MONTH INVITES YOU TO SLOW DOWN AND RECONNECT WITH WHAT TRULY MATTERS.

JANUARY IS YOUR FOUNDATION — A TIME TO GROUND YOUR ENERGY, RETURN TO PRESENCE, AND NOURISH STABILITY.

WITH EACH QUIET MOMENT AND MINDFUL BREATH, YOU CREATE SPACE FOR CLARITY AND RENEWAL.

GRATITUDE BECOMES YOUR ANCHOR, GUIDING YOU GENTLY INTO THE YEAR AHEAD.

JANUARY
MONTH AT A GLANCE
GROUND IN GRATITUDE

January
GROUND IN GRATITUDE

TOP 3 INTENTIONS FOR THE MONTH

_____

_____

_____

_____

AFFIRMATION SPOTLIGHT

"I AM ROOTED IN THE PRESENT MOMENT, SUPPORTED BY PEACE AND GROUNDED IN GRATITUDE."

January
GROUND IN GRATITUDE

REFLECTIONS

RANDOM THOUGHTS

DON'T FORGETS FOR THE MONTH

WHAT GROUNDED ME THE MOST
THIS MONTH?

WHERE DID I FIND MOMENTS OF
STILLNESS OR PEACE?

JANUARY
NOTES & INSIGHTS
GROUND IN GRATITUDE

February

LOVE IN SIMPLICITY

"I CHOOSE LOVE, SIMPLICITY, AND
SOFTNESS IN ALL I DO."

February
LOVE IN SIMPLICITY

MONTHLY FOCUS

FEBRUARY IS A REMINDER TO RETURN TO THE HEART.

THIS MONTH, YOU'RE INVITED TO SLOW YOUR PACE, SOFTEN YOUR EXPECTATIONS, AND LET LOVE WEAVE ITSELF THROUGH DAILY RITUALS.

SIMPLICITY BECOMES A SANCTUARY — A SPACE WHERE CLARITY, COMFORT, AND GRATITUDE NATURALLY RISE.

FEBRUARY
MONTH AT A GLANCE

LOVE IN SIMPLICITY

February

LOVE IN SIMPLICITY

TOP 3 INTENTIONS FOR THE MONTH

_____

_____

_____

_____

_____

AFFIRMATION SPOTLIGHT

"I SOFTEN MY SPIRIT AND ALLOW
LOVE TO FLOW TO ME AND
THROUGH ME WITH EASE."

February
LOVE IN SIMPLICITY

REFLECTIONS

RANDOM THOUGHTS

DON'T FORGETS FOR THE MONTH

WHAT SIMPLE MOMENTS
BROUGHT ME THE MOST JOY?

HOW DID I SHOW MYSELF LOVE
THIS MONTH?

FEBRUARY
NOTES & INSIGHTS
LOVE IN SIMPLICITY

REFLECTION ON MY JOURNEY SO FAR

WHAT SHIFTS HAVE I NOTICED WITHIN MYSELF?

WHAT AM I HEALING, REMEMBERING, OR RELEASING?

WHAT NEW STRENGTHS ARE EMERGING?

HOW HAS MY ENERGY CHANGED?

EVERY STEP FORWARD IS A BECOMING.

March

AWAKEN TO POSSIBILITY

"I OPEN MY HEART TO NEW PERSPECTIVES
AND POSSIBILITIES."

March

AWAKEN TO POSSIBILITY

MONTHLY FOCUS

AS THE WORLD BEGINS TO BLOOM, SO DO YOU. MARCH IS A TIME OF AWAKENING — OF SEEING LIFE WITH FRESH EYES AND WELCOMING NEW IDEAS.

CURIOSITY BECOMES YOUR GUIDE, HELPING YOU NOTICE OPPORTUNITIES AND INSPIRATION THAT WERE ONCE HIDDEN. ALLOW YOUR IMAGINATION TO STRETCH.

MARCH
MONTH AT A GLANCE

AWAKEN TO POSSIBILITY

March

AWAKEN TO POSSIBILITY

TOP 3 INTENTIONS FOR THE MONTH

_____

_____

_____

_____

_____

AFFIRMATION SPOTLIGHT

"I WELCOME NEW PERSPECTIVES, TRUST NEW PATHS, AND AWAKEN TO HIGHER POSSIBILITIES."

March
AWAKEN TO POSSIBILITY

REFLECTIONS

RANDOM THOUGHTS

DON'T FORGETS FOR THE MONTH

WHAT NEW IDEAS OR INSIGHTS
AWAKENED WITHIN ME?

WHERE DID CURIOSITY LEAD ME
THIS MONTH?

MARCH
NOTES & IDEAS

AWAKEN TO POSSIBILITY

QUARTERLY REFLECTION & ALIGNMENT RESET

PAUSE. REFLECT. REALIGN.

WHAT WERE THE BIGGEST LESSONS OF THIS QUARTER?

WHAT AM I PROUD OF MYSELF FOR?

WHERE DID I FEEL THE MOST ALIGNED?

WHERE DID I FEEL RESISTANCE OR BURNOUT?

WHAT HABITS OR BELIEFS AM I READY TO SHIFT?

WHAT DO I WANT TO NURTURE MORE IN THE NEXT QUARTER?

WHAT AM I CALLING IN NEXT?

REFLECTION CREATES CLARITY. CLARITY CREATES ALIGNMENT.

April

TRUST YOUR INTUITION

"MY INTUITION WHISPERS TRUTH;
I AM LEARNING TO LISTEN."

April

TRUST YOUR INTUITION

MONTHLY FOCUS

APRIL CALLS YOU INWARD.

BENEATH THE NOISE OF EVERYDAY LIFE LIES YOUR INNER COMPASS — YOUR INTUITION.

THIS MONTH INVITES YOU TO LISTEN CLOSELY, SLOW DOWN ENOUGH TO HEAR TRUTH, AND TRUST THE GUIDANCE RISING FROM WITHIN.

YOUR INNER KNOWING IS WISE, LOVING, AND ALWAYS LEADING YOU HOME.

APRIL
MONTH AT A GLANCE
TRUST YOUR INTUITION

April

TRUST YOUR INTUITION

TOP 3 INTENTIONS FOR THE MONTH

_____

_____

_____

_____

_____

AFFIRMATION SPOTLIGHT

"MY INNER VOICE IS CLEAR, WISE, AND ALIGNED WITH MY HIGHEST GOOD."

April
TRUST YOUR INTUITION

REFLECTIONS

RANDOM THOUGHTS

DON'T FORGETS FOR THE MONTH

WHEN DID MY INTUITION FEEL
THE STRONGEST THIS MONTH?

HOW DID I MAKE SPACE FOR
INNER CLARITY?

APRIL
NOTES & INSIGHTS
TRUST YOUR INTUITION

REFLECTION ON MY JOURNEY SO FAR

WHAT SHIFTS HAVE I NOTICED WITHIN MYSELF?

WHAT AM I HEALING, REMEMBERING, OR RELEASING?

WHAT NEW STRENGTHS ARE EMERGING?

HOW HAS MY ENERGY CHANGED?

EVERY STEP FORWARD IS A BECOMING.

May

MANIFEST WITH INTENTION

"I ALIGN MY THOUGHTS, WORDS, AND ACTIONS WITH WHAT I DESIRE."

May

MANIFEST WITH INTENTION

MONTHLY FOCUS

MAY IS A MONTH OF CREATION.

THIS IS YOUR MOMENT TO SET CLEAR INTENTIONS, TAKE INSPIRED ACTION, AND MOVE WITH PURPOSE.

MANIFESTATION FLOWS NOT FROM FORCE, BUT FROM ALIGNMENT. WHEN YOU BELIEVE, SPEAK, AND ACT FROM CLARITY — THE PATH OPENS.

MAY
MONTH AT A GLANCE

MANIFEST WITH INTENTION

May

MANIFEST WITH INTENTION

TOP 3 INTENTIONS FOR THE MONTH

_____

_____

_____

_____

_____

AFFIRMATION SPOTLIGHT

"EVERYTHING I DESIRE ALIGNS WITH
ME AS I TAKE INSPIRED AND
INTENTIONAL ACTION."

May

MANIFEST WITH INTENTION

REFLECTIONS

RANDOM THOUGHTS

DON'T FORGETS FOR THE MONTH

_____

_____

_____

WHAT INTENTIONS FELT THE
STRONGEST FOR ME THIS MONTH?

HOW DID I TAKE ALIGNED
ACTION?

_____

_____

_____

_____

_____

_____

MAY
NOTES & MANIFESTATIONS

MANIFEST WITH INTENTION

June

BLOOM INTO ABUNDANCE

"I BLOOM IN ABUNDANCE AND GRATITUDE."

June

BLOOM INTO ABUNDANCE

MONTHLY FOCUS

JUNE IS A CELEBRATION OF GROWTH.

THIS MONTH ENCOURAGES YOU TO OPEN, EXPAND, AND RECEIVE THE ABUNDANCE ALREADY SURROUNDING YOU.

THE MORE GRATITUDE YOU PRACTICE, THE EASIER IT BECOMES TO SEE BEAUTY AND BLESSINGS EVERYWHERE.

LET THIS BE A MONTH OF BLOOMING, INSIDE AND OUT.

JUNE
MONTH AT A GLANCE
BLOOM INTO ABUNDANCE

June

BLOOM INTO ABUNDANCE

TOP 3 INTENTIONS FOR THE MONTH

_____

_____

_____

_____

_____

AFFIRMATION SPOTLIGHT

"I AM OPEN TO RECEIVE ABUNDANCE IN ALL FORMS, AND I TRUST IT FLOWS FREELY TO ME."

June
BLOOM INTO ABUNDANCE

REFLECTIONS

RANDOM THOUGHTS

DON'T FORGETS FOR THE MONTH

WHERE DID I NOTICE ABUNDANCE
THIS MONTH?

WHAT BLESSINGS OR
OPPORTUNITIES SURPRISED ME?

JUNE
NOTES & GRATITUDE LISTS
" BLOOM INTO ABUNDANCE

REFLECTION ON MY JOURNEY SO FAR

WHAT SHIFTS HAVE I NOTICED WITHIN MYSELF?

WHAT AM I HEALING, REMEMBERING, OR RELEASING?

WHAT NEW STRENGTHS ARE EMERGING?

HOW HAS MY ENERGY CHANGED?

EVERY STEP FORWARD IS A BECOMING.

QUARTERLY REFLECTION & ALIGNMENT RESET

PAUSE. REFLECT. REALIGN.

WHAT WERE THE BIGGEST LESSONS OF THIS QUARTER?

WHAT AM I PROUD OF MYSELF FOR?

WHERE DID I FEEL THE MOST ALIGNED?

WHERE DID I FEEL RESISTANCE OR BURNOUT?

WHAT HABITS OR BELIEFS AM I READY TO SHIFT?

WHAT DO I WANT TO NURTURE MORE IN THE NEXT QUARTER?

WHAT AM I CALLING IN NEXT?

REFLECTION CREATES CLARITY. CLARITY CREATES ALIGNMENT.

July

EVOLVE THROUGH EASE

"I RELEASE RESISTANCE AND EVOLVE WITH GRACE."

July
EVOLVE THROUGH EASE

MONTHLY FOCUS

JULY TEACHES THAT GROWTH DOESN'T NEED TO BE HARD.

THIS MONTH, SOFTEN YOUR GRIP. RELEASE THE PRESSURE TO RUSH, PUSH, OR FORCE. EVOLVE GENTLY, NATURALLY, AND WITH TRUST.

WHEN YOU LET EASE LEAD THE WAY, TRANSFORMATION BECOMES FLUID AND INTUITIVE.

JULY
MONTH AT A GLANCE
EVOLVE THROUGH EASE

July

EVOLVE THROUGH EASE

TOP 3 INTENTIONS FOR THE MONTH

_____

_____

_____

_____

_____

July
EVOLVE THROUGH EASE

REFLECTIONS

RANDOM THOUGHTS

DON'T FORGETS FOR THE MONTH

WHERE DID I CHOOSE EASE OVER EFFORT?

WHAT RESISTANCE DID I RELEASE?

JULY
NOTES & REFLECTIONS

EVOLVE THROUGH EASE

August
HEAL & RENEW

"I ALLOW MYSELF TO HEAL, REST, AND RETURN TO WHOLENESS."

August
HEAL & RENEW

MONTHLY FOCUS

AUGUST IS YOUR MONTH OF RESTORATION. REST BECOMES MEDICINE.

STILLNESS BECOMES HEALING. ALLOW YOURSELF TO SLOW DOWN, NURTURE YOUR BODY, AND RESTORE YOUR ENERGY.

RENEWAL COMES WHEN YOU CARE FOR YOURSELF DEEPLY AND WITHOUT GUILT.

AUGUST
MONTH AT A GLANCE
HEAL & RENEW

August

HEAL & RENEW

TOP 3 INTENTIONS FOR THE MONTH

_____

_____

_____

_____

_____

AFFIRMATION SPOTLIGHT

"EVERY BREATH RESTORES ME, AND
EVERY MOMENT INVITES ME BACK
INTO WHOLENESS."

August
HEAL & RENEW

REFLECTIONS

RANDOM THOUGHTS

DON'T FORGETS FOR THE MONTH

WHAT SUPPORTED MY HEALING
THIS MONTH?

WHERE DID I GIVE MYSELF
PERMISSION TO REST?

AUGUST
NOTES & RENEWAL REFLECTIONS

HEAL & RENEW

REFLECTION ON MY JOURNEY SO FAR

WHAT SHIFTS HAVE I NOTICED WITHIN MYSELF?

WHAT AM I HEALING, REMEMBERING, OR RELEASING?

WHAT NEW STRENGTHS ARE EMERGING?

HOW HAS MY ENERGY CHANGED?

EVERY STEP FORWARD IS A BECOMING.

September

CONQUER WITH CONFIDENCE

"I STEP FORWARD BOLDLY, TRUSTING IN MY STRENGTH."

September

CONQUER WITH CONFIDENCE

MONTHLY FOCUS

SEPTEMBER ACTIVATES YOUR COURAGE.

THIS IS A MONTH TO RISE, TAKE RISKS, AND STAND FIRMLY IN YOUR WORTH. CONFIDENCE GROWS THROUGH ACTION — THROUGH SHOWING UP EVEN WHEN UNSURE.

YOUR STRENGTH IS READY TO LEAD YOU FORWARD.

SEPTEMBER
MONTH AT A GLANCE
CONQUER WITH CONFIDENCE

September

CONQUER WITH CONFIDENCE

TOP 3 INTENTIONS FOR THE MONTH

_____

_____

_____

_____

_____

AFFIRMATION SPOTLIGHT

"I RISE WITH COURAGE, SPEAK WITH
CLARITY, AND STEP FORWARD WITH
UNWAVERING CONFIDENCE."

September
CONQUER WITH CONFIDENCE

REFLECTIONS

RANDOM THOUGHTS

DON'T FORGETS FOR THE MONTH

WHERE DID I ACT WITH COURAGE?

WHAT DID I OVERCOME OR MOVE THROUGH?

SEPTEMBER
NOTES & WINS
CONQUER WITH CONFIDENCE

October

RISE IN POWER

"I HONOR MY BOUNDARIES AND MY BRILLIANCE."

October
RISE IN POWER

MONTHLY FOCUS

OCTOBER INVITES YOU INTO EMPOWERED EMBODIMENT.

THIS MONTH IS ABOUT OWNING YOUR TRUTH, PROTECTING YOUR ENERGY, AND ELEVATING YOUR VOICE.

STAND TALL. SET BOUNDARIES WITH CLARITY. LEAD FROM YOUR INNER STRENGTH AND WISDOM.

OCTOBER
MONTH AT A GLANCE

RISE IN POWER

October
RISE IN POWER

TOP 3 INTENTIONS FOR THE MONTH

_____

_____

_____

_____

October

RISE IN POWER

REFLECTIONS

RANDOM THOUGHTS

DON'T FORGETS FOR THE MONTH

HOW DID I HONOR MY
BOUNDARIES?

WHERE DID I RISE INSTEAD OF
SHRINK?

REFLECTION ON MY JOURNEY SO FAR

WHAT SHIFTS HAVE I NOTICED WITHIN MYSELF?

WHAT AM I HEALING, REMEMBERING, OR RELEASING?

WHAT NEW STRENGTHS ARE EMERGING?

HOW HAS MY ENERGY CHANGED?

EVERY STEP FORWARD IS A BECOMING.

November

EMBODY JOY

"I LIVE JOYFULLY, FULLY, AND IN ALIGNMENT."

November
EMBODY JOY

MONTHLY FOCUS

NOVEMBER CELEBRATES JOY AS A WAY OF BEING.

THIS MONTH INVITES MORE PLAY, PRESENCE, LAUGHTER, AND CONNECTION. JOY EXPANDS WHEN SHARED — AND WHEN CHOSEN INTENTIONALLY.

EMBODY THE FULLNESS OF WHO YOU ARE.

NOVEMBER
MONTH AT A GLANCE

EMBODY JOY

November

EMBODY JOY

TOP 3 INTENTIONS FOR THE MONTH

_____

_____

_____

_____

_____

AFFIRMATION SPOTLIGHT

"JOY FLOWS THROUGH EVERY PART OF MY LIFE, AND I ALLOW MYSELF TO FULLY EXPERIENCE IT."

November

EMBODY JOY

REFLECTIONS

RANDOM THOUGHTS

DON'T FORGETS FOR THE MONTH

WHAT BROUGHT ME JOY THIS MONTH?

HOW DID I STAY PRESENT AND GRATEFUL?

NOVEMBER
NOTES & JOY REFLECTIONS
EMBODY JOY

December

CELEBRATE YOUR BECOMING

"I HONOR HOW FAR I'VE COME AND TRUST WHAT'S AHEAD."

December

CELEBRATE YOUR BECOMING

MONTHLY FOCUS

DECEMBER IS A SACRED PAUSE — A MOMENT TO REFLECT, CELEBRATE, AND HONOR YOUR GROWTH.

EVERY LESSON, EVERY BREAKTHROUGH, EVERY STEP HAS SHAPED THE PERSON YOU ARE TODAY.

LET THIS MONTH BE FILLED WITH GRATITUDE, CLOSURE, AND HOPE FOR THE NEXT CHAPTER.

DECEMBER
MONTH AT A GLANCE
CELEBRATE YOUR BECOMING

December

CELEBRATE YOUR BECOMING

TOP 3 INTENTIONS FOR THE MONTH

_____

_____

_____

_____

_____

AFFIRMATION SPOTLIGHT

"I HONOR MY JOURNEY, CELEBRATE
MY GROWTH, AND TRUST THE
BEAUTY UNFOLDING AHEAD."

December
CELEBRATE YOUR BECOMING

REFLECTIONS

RANDOM THOUGHTS

DON'T FORGETS FOR THE MONTH

WHAT AM I MOST PROUD OF
FROM THIS YEAR?

WHAT CHAPTERS AM I READY TO
CLOSE?

DECEMBER
REFLECTIONS & YEAR-END GRATITUDE

CELEBRATE YOUR BECOMING

YEAR-END REFLECTION:
A YEAR OF BECOMING

WHAT SURPRISED ME THE MOST ABOUT MYSELF?

WHAT AM I MOST PROUD OF?

WHAT CHALLENGED ME AND SHAPED ME?

WHAT DID I HEAL?

WHAT AM I RELEASING BEFORE THE NEW YEAR?

WHAT BLESSINGS DO I WANT TO CARRY FORWARD?

CELEBRATE YOUR BECOMING.

YEAR-END REFLECTION:
A YEAR OF BECOMING

REFLECT. RELEASE. RENEW.

TAKE A MOMENT TO CELEBRATE YOUR YEAR — EVERY BREAKTHROUGH, EVERY QUIET WIN,
EVERY STEP THAT BROUGHT YOU CLOSER TO YOURSELF.

"YOUR EVOLUTION IS EVIDENCE OF GRACE."

"GRATITUDE FOR WHAT WAS"   **"HOPE FOR WHAT'S TO COME"**

MY INTENTION:

WHY THIS INTENTION MATTERS TO ME:

HOW I WANT TO FEEL IN THE NEXT CHAPTER:

WHAT I AM CALLING IN:

WHAT I AM READY TO RELEASE:

YEAR-END REFLECTION:
A YEAR OF BECOMING

DEAR SOUL,

THANK YOU FOR SAYING YES TO YOUR JOURNEY —
FOR SHOWING UP, FOR HEALING, FOR CHOOSING PRESENCE.

YOU'VE DONE SOMETHING TRULY BEAUTIFUL THIS YEAR: YOU'VE COME
HOME TO YOURSELF. THE WORLD SHIFTS EVERY TIME ONE PERSON
AWAKENS TO THEIR JOY. SO AS YOU STEP FORWARD, REMEMBER —
YOU ARE THE LIGHT YOU'VE BEEN CULTIVATING.

KEEP SHINING, KEEP GROUNDING, KEEP BECOMING.

WITH INFINITE GRATITUDE AND LOVE,
JOY HAFNER
FOUNDER OF TRUEJOY LIVING

*"MAY YOU WALK INTO EVERY NEW SEASON GROUNDED IN GRATITUDE, GUIDED
BY INTUITION, AND GLOWING WITH JOY."*